# MY SISTERS
By Allan Ishmael Young

MY SISTERS

# MY SISTERS

by Allan Ishmael Young

## PREFACE

Alas and alack! My sisters were as different as night and day—they did not look alike, act alike, or like the same things.

I admired Stella's raucous approach of grabbing whatever life handed her by the horns and running with it, or wrestling it to the ground, if necessary.

But I also envied Ruth's quiet taciturn approach to everything that beset her in life, and her ability to accept or ignore it—whatever suited her mood at the time.

Stella was a blond towhead, like me, and we both had our father's bright blue eyes.

Ruth had the mysterious dark eyes and hair of our "Black Irish" mother—as did our brother.

Stella was not a reader for pleasure, although she was an excellent student in school.

Ruth was the silent introverted reader, who liked to sew, cook, and who didn't mind housework.

Stella disliked anything to do with housework, but loved being outside in the garden—or even in the hills and woods with me, in our early years.

Ruth would do anything to avoid having to work outside in the yard or garden.

Stella tried to do many active things, even learning to ice skate at almost age thirty, after moving to an area where there was ice.

Ruth disliked physical activity, and would even stop her chores to read something that caught her eye.

Stella liked "*Your Hit Parade*" on the radio, and sometimes stayed home on Saturday nights to listen to it.

Ruth preferred country music—and married a guy who played it very well on guitar and mandolin.

Stella knew that our overly-religious mother frowned on the girls wearing anything except dresses or skirts, because everything else was unladylike. She not only wore slacks, but shorts and swimsuits too. And why not—she was built like the proverbial brick outhouse

Ruth was built the same way, but did not show it. She made a lot of her own clothes, and didn't seem to mind following our mother's dictums about clothing.

After Stella went to work, she showed a preference for matching shoes and purses—getting new ones often.

I have to admit I did not write as much about Ruth herein as I did Stella, because I did not know her as well.

# Part I
# STELLA'S STORY

# STELLA'S STORY, by Allan Ishmael Young

## Chapter 1, STELLA'S CHILDHOOD

Stella May Young was born in the same house I was born in at Black Mountain coal camp on May 6, 1925. The camp name was later changed to Bonny Blue, after Blue Diamond Coal Company bought the Black Mountain operation.

My first memory of her was when she helped me learn to read and write—and talk! Yes, TALK! I stuttered. Yep, I made Mel Tillis sound like Winston Churchill.

When I was four years old my family would become so frustrated with me trying to tell them something that they would scream at me. My little brother and I sat on a big wooden box to eat. A box which our dad had absconded with from the coal mine company where he worked. We were poor. Our parents had chairs, and our two older sisters had stools made by our dad from scrap lumber, but my brother and I ate sitting on a box.

One night at the supper table, I was trying to tell something and, as usual, the words wouldn't come. The ones that did were horribly mangled.

My father suddenly yelled, "Spit it out, Ignuts!"

Then he backhanded me across the mouth, knocking me off the box to the floor, while everyone else laughed. Being a hungry kid, I crawled back up on the box to continue eating. Stella was the only family member that showed any sympathy for my plight. Maybe my other siblings were too afraid to.

As time went on, I quit trying to talk—became surly and pouty. Then I decided to cure my stuttering. My mom used lye to clean the old wood floors in our Kemmerer Gem coal camp house, so I ate some—figuring it would make my mouth work. It didn't. Fortunately I didn't swallow any, but it messed up my lips. I couldn't eat for days, and begged my mom for food. "Just one little bean," I would say, to satisfy the gnawing pain in my little belly. But the doctor said no. So I became even more surly, and wouldn't talk at all.

But Stella got me to playing school with her, long before I was old enough to attend school myself. She would pretend to be a teacher most of the time, but she liked for me to help her with her homework, too. I enjoyed it, even when she laughed at my mistakes—because I was learning to talk right. Like the day I was reading her spelling words to her, and she spelled them back to me. I read "deetermine," and she laughed and pronounced it correctly.

"That's a fifth-grade word, anyway," she said.

So Stella and I cemented our sibling friendship through such activities.

I can barely remember other family activities before this. Our mother always dragged me along to the company store, shopping, leaving the two girls home with the baby. Once Stella was scolded severely for trying to take him for a ride in her baby buggy. She dropped him, and somehow he got his finger caught in the buggy's wheel, and hurt it. Mom thought it was broken, but it wasn't.

Both my sisters had gotten fancy dolls and doll buggies for Christmas. Ruth still had hers many years later, but non-domestic Stella had dragged her doll up and down the creek bank by one leg until there was nothing left. I do not know what ever happened to her buggy. She preferred different types of toys.

Our dad had told us much about his pet goats he had acquired when he was a boy, although he was put to work in the mines at age nine. He had built a wagon for them to pull in harness, and had even made the harness.

Now he proceeded to do that again. He traded something for a goat somewhere, and built a brightly-colored wagon for it to pull. I was too little to drive it, but Stella loved it. We would even ride the wagon all the way to Grandma's house in

Wagner Town, below St. Charles. Dad walked alongside, of course, with a line tied to the goat's collar, just in case. The goat foraged in the mountains for food, but came home every evening for food scraps at home.

Stella and I were much alike, both being towheads—and having our father's blue eyes. Our older sister, Ruth, and the baby, L.B., had inherited our mom's dark hair and almost black eyes of her ancestors, the Black Irish.

At about this time our mom became severely ill. She was taken to the hospital in Norton, and our dad was told she would not recover. But she did. I never knew what her illness was. During this time my brother, who was just barely out of diapers, and I stayed with our grandmother and Aunt Jess in St. Charles, while Ruth and Stella stayed with Mom's childless half-sister, Dixie, and her husband, John Hendricks. During this period Uncle John, or "Bud," as we called him, developed a liking for Stella, whom he called "May," her middle name. He took her many places. Since our dad had no car, we kids never went anyplace we couldn't walk.

Several times I came back into our kitchen after supper to find Ruth and Stella quarreling. I finally figured it out. Ruth washed dishes, at a very early age, and Stella dried them. But Stella couldn't dry until they were washed, and Ruth was a piddler. Slow in everything she did, and prone to stop and read something that caught her eye—even the newspapers which Mom used on the walls to thwart the winter winds. Stella wanted to get the dish washing chore over and done with, so she could get on to other activities. What it boiled down to was that she didn't like housework, preferring to be outside. Ruth was just the opposite—she would do anything to get to stay in the house.

The depression was in full swing, but as kids we did not know that. Dad got in a day or so at the shut-down mines occasionally, keeping the pumps running, to remove water from the mines. For food, he plowed up a large "newground" in a hollow high up on coal company land, fenced it, and raised much garden produce. He used a hoe to dig into the hillside near the gate to the garden, and produced a spring of free-flowing cold water. Such a delight, after digging in the garden for a while, to lie on your stomach to get a long cold drink! Stella and I were his "assistant gardeners," spending a lot of time in that garden, helping to plant, hoe and harvest. Our brother, "Bee," was too small, and Ruth hated that kind of work. Dad also acquired a milk cow, which, wearing an identifying bell, foraged in the mountains for food, like the goat, but came home every evening to be fed and milked night and morning. Using scrap lumber from the mines, Dad built a small shed in our back yard for the cow and goat. Also, he built a small pig pen on the bluff behind our house, where we housed a hog for meat every year. With our cow's milk, our garden produce, butchered hogs, and what game Dad shot in the mountains, we ate pretty good.

Another of our jobs was to carry water to the hog every day. There was a nice clear pool in the small spring-fed creek that ran down the hill and into the big creek. One day, as we approached it with our buckets, several kids whose last name was Phipps, seeing what we were about to do, ran ahead of us and stomped around in the pool, muddying the water. We had to wait until it cleared somewhat, before we could get our buckets full. Then they did it again!

This became an almost daily entertainment for them, when they would spot us heading for the pool. Later that summer their alcoholic father ran his car off the road down in the Gap of the Mountain, killing himself and a friend. In spite of the outpouring of grief for his children by others, Stella and I felt no sympathy for them.

In 1936, when Stella was eleven years old and I was eight, our twenty-one-year-old cousin, Clarence, was shot and killed. Since where he lived, with his brother Howard, who was twelve, his mother and our grandmother, had no electricity, the wake or "sittin' up," as it was more commonly known, was held at our house in Kemmerer Gem coal camp. It consisted of a twenty-four hour vigil for three days. Many people came and went, including a lot of relatives we had never seen before. Stella spent a lot of time getting to know the other kids her age.

My sister was a sentimentalist, but with enough ingrained humor and mischief to keep those in her world happy. At our home the cats were always hers, but when one of them died, she would bury it in a shoebox, then pick violets and daisies for days, putting them on its grave, while sitting there on the grass with tears in her big beautiful blue eyes. Over the years I saw lots of tears in those eyes, but never for herself—always for someone or something else.

Then in August of that year our dad bought a three-roomed house on a small piece of land in the country at the base of Elk Knob. Having spent almost all of his life in coal camps, he said he wanted to get a breath of air somebody else had not already breathed. From this house we could see many miles down the valley towards the county seat, Jonesville, as well as all the surrounding ridges and mountains—some close, some far away. Stella loved living out there, working in the gardens, and reading while swinging in one of the two front porch swings which Dad built.

## Chapter 2, STELLA'S SCHOOLING

Before we moved to the country, our house in the coal camp, like all the camp houses, had a big front porch, which almost reached to the road. There couldn't have been more than two or three vehicles a day came by on that road, but we spent a lot of time playing on the porch and watching the cars and trucks go by anyway. A great place for small children to play, or grownups to do some household work. When I was about four years old, a young man named Hershel Parsons was doing some repair work on our house about this time, and ran in on our front porch one day to get out of the rain.

I was to learn later that his father had been killed in the mine, the company was helping him attend Virginia Polytechnic Institute, and he worked in the camp in summer. Later he became one of the first P-38 pilots.

This rainy day he asked me if I had anything he could read to me. I guess he just wanted to keep from being bored. Nobody had ever read to me. My mother had finished seventh grade, but all she read was the Bible. My father finished second grade, and couldn't read at all. I scrounged around and found a reader belonging to one of my older sisters. Hershel started reading Beowulf. I was fascinated, and couldn't get enough. But the rain stopped, and he had to go back to work.

That fall I was playing in our coal pile out by the front fence, in lieu of a sandbox, when a nice red-haired lady came walking by and kidded me about being a coal miner. I learned she went to teach at someplace called "school," and walked by our house every morning and afternoon. One day she asked if I would like to visit there sometime.

So the next day my mother dressed me all up in clean overalls and shirt, and I hiked off to "school," a simple one-room building just a few houses up the road from our home, with Miss Pennington. She had a desk up on a stage at the front of the room, and told me I could sit on the edge of the stage, since all the seats were occupied. Soon both my older sisters showed up. I had known they got dressed and went off somewhere every morning, but had no idea where they went. I don't think they approved of me being there. Suddenly older kids I knew, including my sisters, were reading—just like Hershel Parsons had done for me! I was fascinated.

She sent me home at recess, but the next day I was back again. And every day, until I was old enough to start school myself the following year. I convinced myself I could learn to read like that, so I gritted my little baby teeth, talked real slow, pronouncing each word very carefully, though sometimes wrong. My youngest sister, Stella, three years older than I, had noticed my fascination with school on my first day there, and right away started playing school with me. She would read to me, and sometimes show me words to read myself, so that by the time I started school the following year, I knew the alphabet, could count to ten, and write my name. I'm sure Stella never realized how much she helped me. By then, the school had been doubled in size, so there were two rooms. Miss Pennington taught the higher level classes, and a new teacher, Miss Fannon, taught the lower grades, including me. Since Stella was in a higher grade, we didn't sit in the same room.

At the school in Kemmerer Gem it was a privilege to be asked, or told, to take the blackboard erasers out and dust them—usually against the side of the building. But you felt like a king when given the responsibility of burning the waste paper. The wastebaskets in each room were of wire mesh, and to a primer first year student, like me, they seemed enormous. Even bigger were the ones over on the creek bank in which the paper was burned. One windy day my friend Willard Freels and I were told to do this chore, so we ran the handles of two brooms through the wastebasket and carried it between us to the burn area. When the wind started to blow the burning paper out of the containers, we swatted at it with our brooms, setting them on fire. The teacher, Miss Fannon, swatted us five times with her paddle, as punishment for destroying the brooms. I was humiliated! We couldn't help what happened on the creek bank.

Sitting at home later, pouting, I was asked what was wrong by Stella.

When I told her, she said, "Miss Pennington wouldn't have spanked you. She would have understood. All teachers are not like Miss Pennington."

I learned she was right.

My sister had a lot of empathy for everybody. On one Valentines Day, when so many kids got cards from others, she came home with me at noon with sad tears in her eyes.

When I asked what was wrong, she said, "Every kid in school got at least one valentine card, except Alfred Phipps. I really wish I had put one in the box for him."

I knew that Alfred was a pretty good kid, even though he was the brother of the ones who muddied up our hog water spring. But for some reason he was somewhat of an outcast. I had noticed the year before, when I sat on Miss Pennington's stage, that he sat alone in his double seat, and talked to himself quite a bit.

Later, after we returned to school after lunch, a happy Stella hunted me up on the playground.

"Alfred got a valentine," she said, smiling. "I think the teacher gave him one."

That sounded like something Miss Pennington, or Stella if she had another card, would do.

School started at the Elk Knob School soon after we moved there, and I was surprised to learn that neighbor Brad Johnson, although he was Stella's age, was in my grade, the third. Our grades consisted of a primer for the first year, then eleven numbered grades. Stella attended Elk Knob School from fifth through seventh. I started there in third grade. Although she and I were three years apart in age, we became two years apart in school, since I had taken primer and first grade both in one year at Kemmerer Gem.

A summer recreational program was started at the school the following year, which she and I enjoyed. The county provided two teachers, one for kids under twelve, and one for those older. We worked on projects, played games, went on picnics, and took hiking trips up in the Knob. Quite enjoyable for bored country kids when there was no school, and both Stella and I became bored quite easily.

After Stella finished seventh grade, she started high school at Pennington. The school bus delivered kids to Elk Knob School, then took a load to the high school—including her. We still walked to school together in the morning, but by the time she got back to Elk Knob School in the evening, I was already home. I didn't really learn much about her high school activities, so when I started there two years later, I had no idea what to expect.

She did seem to enjoy high school, and was involved in several in-school activities. Like in grade school, she was always the student with the best grades in her class. She did get to finally see a movie. The teachers treated all the students to one for Christmas.

None of the schools we attended had a lunch program. Students had to bring their own, or go home to eat. Of course in grade school we went home, since it was near enough—but there were many empty paper bags in all the waste baskets, and some on the ground. When I joined her in high school two years later, she told me she would fix our lunches, if I would carry them. So every day she sought me out at my locker, took her sandwiches or apple and walked away with her friends. I always had a full paper bag in my hand on the morning bus, and a folded paper bag in my pocket on the afternoon bus. Our system worked well for the two years we were in high school together.

I had begun to realize what a beautiful girl she was when she started high school. She always dressed as sharp as our circumstances allowed, and her naturally blond hair was always neatly cared for. We were talking in the hall one day when one of the senior boys cornered me later. He asked me if I knew that pretty junior. When I said yes, he told me she was the most delightful and confident girl in school. He said he had been given the task of gathering a team of students and inventorying the books in the library. He said Stella had stepped in with enthusiasm, took over part of his load, and cheerfully helped until the job was done.

She liked to introduce me to her friends as her "Big Brother," sounding like I was the oldest. Of course I was taller than her. Some of her friends must have taken her seriously, because sometimes I was plagued by the friendship of girls in her grade, and being young and dumb, I didn't really know what to do about them.

Stella was constantly a straight-A student, liked school, and studied before and after riding the bus to school and back home. Then when she graduated in 1943, she was obviously insulted. The two top students in her class were Stella and Anna Ruth Jessee, the daughter of the Pennington Chevrolet dealer. After seeing all the grades, the principal, Robert E. Beeler, Jr., sent the two girls around to all their teachers to get their grades for the last half of their senior year, so he could decide who would be the valedictorian and the second level salutatorian. The last teacher they approached was English teacher Martha Gibson Barron. Obvious to the girls, when Mrs. Barron saw that Stella was in the lead, she gave Anna Ruth a 98 for the period, and Stella an 88. Stella had never gotten an 88 in her life! But she had to give the graduation speech, while Anna Ruth basked in the warmth of her unearned title. None of my siblings had ever liked Mrs.

Barron, but I got along with her because she was the director of our plays and musicals, in which I participated. But I never saw her the same way after that.

But the night of graduation everybody in that auditorium could readily tell who was the smartest girl in that class. Stella wrote her own speech. Two of them, in fact. The principal insisted on reviewing and approving what she was going to say. And she gave him a copy. But it was not the one she presented! The one she presented could have been written by a forty-five-year-old college professor. She compared high school experiences to life in general, and finally gave credit to all the teachers who had helped her, mentioning their names. I noticed that she had deliberately omitted the principal and Mrs. Barron, as I watched the pleased smiles on the faces of the ones she mentioned. The applause was thunderous. You could see it in people's eyes, the wonder as to who this vastly intelligent high school senior was, who knew so much about their lives. I don't imagine that very many people there that night remembered the name of either of the girls who were the valedictorian and salutatorian, but I'll bet many of them remembered that speech for a long time.

I heard later that the principal became furious the next day, after her talk soaked in. But Stella and her diploma were long gone.

## Chapter 3, STELLA'S ENTERTAINMENT

The spring when Stella was about eight years old, she showed me an advertisement in a magazine about how you could earn a guitar by selling garden seeds. She desperately wanted that guitar, so, in spite of our parents discouraging her, she sent for the seeds. She worked her butt off for weeks, peddling seed envelopes all over the coal camp. And she finally got enough sold to earn the guitar. Her dismay was shared by all her siblings and friends, when the guitar turned out to be made of cardboard, and wasn't much bigger than a ukulele! But our neighbors, Everett and Geneva Long, had a niece visiting, who could play a guitar. She proceeded to tune Stella's instrument pretty well, and picked quite a few tunes on it, while teaching Stella some chords—so Stella's disappointment was somewhat diffused.

Entertainment for coal camp kids was practically nil, unless they created it themselves. They could head for St. Charles for the "show," as moving pictures were called, on Saturday nights—that is, if they had a dime. Our own mother, being overly-religious, considered the show sinful. Consequently, Stella never saw a show until she was in high school, where the teachers rewarded all students with a trip to the movies for Christmas. She saw such pictures as Gone with the Wind, Shepherd of the Hills, and Trail of the Lonesome Pine that way. But in the coal camps, kids were somewhat on their own, when it came to amusements. Our own dad hung a tire swing from the limb of a tree across the creek in back of our house, on which Stella spent many happy hours. Also, there were several grapevine swings in the hills, cut by the bigger boys. In front of our house was a street light—a bulb and reflector hanging on a utility pole. Some of the bigger kids hung a long sturdy rope from the pole, and in the evening, many kids, boys and girls alike, enjoyed "jump rope" there—including Stella.

But sometimes her tomboyishness caused trouble, for both her and her siblings. She always wanted to do what the boys around the neighborhood did, whether she could or not. Once Dad used some scrap lumber to make a small boat for myself and Bee. He attached a rope to it, and we could pull it around in a shallow pond in the creek behind our house. One day we went out to play with it, and Stella, who was afraid of water, and her obnoxious friend and neighbor, Edith Jones, were sitting in the boat in the back yard, one in each end, rocking it back and forth like a rocky horse.

When we demanded that they relinquish it to us, they laughed and refused. When our high-tempered Dad heard the ruckus, he came out with an axe, and turned the boat into kindling.

Earl Carter was the camp maintenance man, and kept a team of horses and a wagon as part of his paraphernalia. One Saturday afternoon, apparently Earl Carter was gone, because up the camp road came his wagon, loaded with kids, and pulled by a gang of teenage boys. Stella and I were on our front porch, and her eyes really lit up. I could see she would give anything to join that group—but we both knew that our safety-first mother would not let us. Still, it looked like a lot of fun. Of course, Stella, who was a close friend of Earl's youngest daughter, let me know that Earl was pretty upset when he learned about it.

Our mother felt the same way about the home made merry-go-rounds built by the older kids. They consisted of a cross-tie or similar piece of timber set in the ground, like a post, then a spike driven into the exposed end, and a long sturdy board mounted over the spike, on the two ends of which several kids could sit. Then someone had to spin the board, ducking under it as it went around.

Stella liked hiking in the wooded hills with me, especially when the leaves were at their colorful best in the fall. One day she and I were crawling through a barbed wire fence near our home when she ripped a big gash in her knee on the fence. It bled profusely, and left a big permanent scar. She didn't seem to be bothered by the scar. She had been born with a large chocolate-colored birthmark on the back of her right calf muscle, which also didn't seem to bother her. I have no idea if such things were hereditary, but our dad had one on his shoulder, and cousin Howard had one on his chest.

When our cousin Howard's brother died, by the third day of the "sittin' up," many young people were getting weary, or bored, and becoming restless. Stella took it on herself to entertain them. She took them on a hike to Old Darby mine, where later we found and harvested some mistletoe. My cousin Harry and I were not invited; too young, I guess, but we followed, since I knew the way. But when we arrived at the mine, we saw no one, and wondered where else they could have gone. Just as he and I approached the driftmouth of the mine, here came a coal car drifting rapidly down the track out of the mine—loaded with screaming teenagers and pre-teens. Stella and friends and relatives had pushed the thing far into the abandoned mine, and since the track had a slope on the way out, they were coasting down.

Leave it to Stella to come up with such entertainment. Well, she might have had a little help from her cousin Howard, with whom she had become close friends. Their friendship lasted the rest of their lives. But on that day, riding the car on successive trips kept everybody excited. They even let Harry and me join them.

Stella's activities were conducive to her wearing more appropriate attire than a dress or skirt, but Mom frowned on slacks, much less shorts. So the girls were forbidden to wear them. Unladylike, our mother said.

We never had a Christmas tree in the coal camp house. Mom would put up several red and green crepe paper decorations, swung from the ceiling of the living room. On Christmas Eve each of us kids put a shoebox under our bed, and next morning it would contain a toy, plus some candy, nuts and perhaps an apple or an orange. One year Dad asked Stella and me if we knew about mistletoe. We told him yes, but we had never seen any. He said he knew where there was some, and asked if we wanted to go get it. So we hiked up an old wagon road to Old Darby mine, which had been worked out and abandoned.

Standing on the hillside, next to the driftmouth of the mine, were several trees. In the forks of the trees were growing bunches of plants. Dad told us that mistletoe was a parasite plant which grew on others that way. The bunches were too high up for us to reach, and the trees could not be climbed because they had no lower limbs. Dad proceeded to unlimber his shotgun, which he had thoughtfully brought along, and simply shot several bunches of mistletoe from the crotches of the trees, which Stella and I picked up and put into bags we had brought. It not only contributed to the decorations around home, but she took some to school, also.

Holidays were the occasions for our Grandma, her daughter Jess, and Jess' son, our cousin, Howard, to visit. He was a year older than Stella, but they were great friends. Dad would drive to wherever they lived and bring them to our country place on Easter, the fourth of July and Christmas. On the fourth of July Dad would order in advance three gallons of ice cream, one each of vanilla, chocolate and strawberry. Stella and I preferred the strawberry. Then one year Dad traded for a worn out ice cream maker, and got it to working. Stella, Howard and I turned the crank until each of us was worn out, then Dad mounted an electric motor on it, to relieve the human power.

I knew nothing about Christmas trees, never having had one, but the first Christmas after we moved to the country, Stella wanted me to go with her to get one. We took a small saw and an axe, and went down in Trig Stamper's pasture, which was dotted with small cedar trees. We selected one we liked, cut it and took it home. Dad nailed two cross pieces of lumber to its trunk so it would stand up. My two sisters made all kinds of homemade decorations out of paper, string, popcorn and stuff. It really looked nice.

Stella and Howard always found many things to do together on these occasions—many of them helpful or entertaining for the gathering. Howard liked to sprawl on the bed with all of us kids and tell ghost stories—and he told them as if they happened to him. Sometimes Stella could not sleep later, she was so scared, and she was easily scared. Once I got even with her for a dirty trick she played on me by scaring her.

She wanted me to do something for her that I didn't want to do. She promised me a pair of white socks if I would, so I complied with her wishes. We were so poor that any gift of clothing was appreciated. Later I learned she didn't have a pair of white socks. She "socked" me with her fists two times. That bugged this little boy immensely. Such a disappointment. Later when she went to the neighbor's well for two buckets of drinking water, she had to walk past our barn. I sneaked down to the barn, hid in a back stall, and when she came along, I began groaning and moaning horribly. I couldn't see what happened to her, but when I came back to the house, she and Mom were livid. Stella had run all the way home, spilling all her water.

Although she and I were a lot alike, and good friends for a brother and sister, she liked to pick on me whenever she could. After I learned how easily frightened she was, I would get even by scaring her. Dad had put a light on a pole over the entrance to the cellar, which shined all over the back yard. The switch was inside the house. When Stella would go to the outhouse at night, she would leave the light on and the toilet door open. If Mom wasn't looking, sometimes I would flip the switch to turn the light off. This would bring Stella running into the house, screaming, and pulling her clothes on as she ran. By then I would be somewhere else, so no one knew who flipped the switch—but she always guessed it was me.

Stella was not very athletic, although the Elk Knob school sponsored a girls' basketball team, which played on a hard-packed clay outdoor court, and a boys' softball team. Both our teams played against other similar schools in the county. She didn't go out for basketball, because Mom wouldn't have let her wear in public the short shorts the girls wore. I didn't play softball because I could not afford a glove. (My brother and I played catch at home using stuffed paper bags to protect our hands.) Our parents believed strictly in the three R's—no extracurricular activities. Although I did get involved in school plays, where no investment was needed.

During our Elk Knob years I learned how much Stella liked to play games on the floor, such as "Jacks," or "Jack Rocks," as it was sometimes called. She taught me to play it, and I got to be pretty good at it— but never as good as she was. The object of the game was to bounce a small rubber ball in the air while sitting on the floor, and then to pick up a number of the "Rocks" while the ball bounced, then retrieve the ball. The number of rocks picked up went in succession, from one to however many were in the pile. At first we really used rocks, or small gravels, because we couldn't afford the regular jacks that came in a set with a ball. Later I think someone got her a set of jacks for Christmas. I could never get her to play "Mumble Peg" with me, pretty much a boys' game involving flipping a knife. She disliked anything that resembled a weapon. Most boys had pocket knives at this stage of our lives. We wore high-top lace-up boots, and most of them came with a knife pocket near the top of one of them, and a Barlow pocket knife came with it.

Over time all we siblings learned to play checkers and Chinese checkers, after acquiring the equipment to do so. Of course our first checker board was homemade, and our checkers were pop bottle caps, carried off from the nearby general store.

Stella and I made our own kites, by using paste made from flour and water, and scrounged all the store twine we could—tying several pieces together for a great length. Stella loved to join me in a neighboring field to watch the kite flutter in the wind. We would wrap the string around a Karo syrup bucket for ease of winding it up, then one of us would sit on the bucket to hold it down.

None of us kids got to go to any staged entertainment, but later our Uncle John and Aunt Dixie went to the Ringling Brothers Barnum and Bailey Circus in Bristol, and took Ruth and Stella with them.

Stella and Ruth both liked to dress up and go to church with our mother—which, for them, was a form of entertainment, too. It gave them a chance to show off new clothing, and to meet other people.

I do not remember Stella attending any parties when we were in grade school or high school. Our mother frowned on such things. But after she went to work at Oak Ridge, almost 150 miles away, near Knoxville, it seemed like every time she came home, she would head for a party in one of the coal camp homes—usually in the mining camp of Benedict. Our mother did not object, or if she did, I did not know about it. I think the parties were put on by other Oak Ridge workers who were home at the same time as Stella. My orders from our dad were to take her wherever she wanted to go, since she did not drive. This became even more prevalent after Dad became less able to work, and Stella was helping the family more. I had nothing in common with the attendees of these parties, so I would drop her off, then come back later. But most of the time, when I went back to get her, she would be taken home by some guy at the party.

One night we were heading for such a party, when about halfway between Woodway and Pennington, our car quit. At about age sixteen, I knew little mechanically about cars—but I boldly raised the hood, expecting the engine to be absent. At that time a car full of young people came along, stopped and asked where we were going. Before I had time to answer, Stella blurted out the name and address of the party. The driver of the car said that was where they were heading. So Stella got in with them, wished me luck with the car, and rode away. All I could do was walk the two miles or so back home, expecting Dad to be really upset. But he wasn't. It was almost like he had been expecting this. The next day he and I walked down to the car, he figured out what was wrong with it, and we hitched a ride to Pennington to get a part for it. That night I was driving Stella to another party—with a certain amount of apprehension, of course.

Even after having children Stella liked to do different things. After moving to Iowa she enjoyed going to the state park beaches with her boys, even though it was not her husband's thing. She went on extended hikes in the colorful forests in fall, and even tried ice skating with her sons.

One of her prime entertainments—a hobby really—was growing African violets in her basement. They were all over the place.

## Chapter 4, STELLA'S FRIENDS

Across the road from our place at Elk Knob lived a widow named Rose Johnson, with one daughter and four sons still at home. Her youngest son, Bradley, who was Stella's age, would pick his banjo and sing on their front porch in the evening.

One night Stella said, "I wonder what that is that that old boy is playing."

Dad said, "Sounds like he is playing hell, to me!"

Brad and Stella became good friends. Stella, a straight-A fifth grader, was soon surrounded by many new friends, including Delephine Scarborough, a scrawny girl Stella's age who lived with two old bachelor uncles near us, and she and Stella walked back and forth to school together. At Dot, a crossroads a mile east of us, there was a store run by a family named Ervin, who had one child, a dark haired blue eyed daughter my age named Emma Kate. Stella was often invited to their house to play with the lonely Emma Kate, especially on holidays—and she would go, but reluctantly, because that was when our own relatives would visit us.

Some of her tales about her school mates were hilarious. One day she came home from school laughing at an incident involving a classmate of hers named Velma Myers. (Or was her name Velda? I do not remember.) Anyway, the girl asked the teacher if she could "go be excused." (Yep, that's what we all said when we wanted to go to the school's outhouse. We didn't ask to be excused, but to "go be excused!") The teacher told the girl she would have to wait until their current class was over. Stella said Velma stood up and screamed, "I've got to shit!" Girls were not supposed to talk like that, but I guess desperation could drive a person to do it.

Another of her close friends was Evelyn Fleenor, who even at an early age played piano in church for funerals and such. Evelyn was a redhead Stella's age. They had matching builds, and were the same size. Some people thought they were sisters. Evelyn, too, seemed to have a lot of empathy for others, as did Stella. Brad Johnson chased both of them, as did other guys—but Stella showed no interest in Brad. Evelyn later married him—had to, I heard, and they had two sons.

I was to learn how much Stella was growing up. She was starting to think about boys a lot. When Dad still worked at Kemmerer Gem Coal Company we would still go there often. This night there was a box supper at the school house there, and we went. Dad liked bidding against Lee Hedgecoth (Stella's future father-in-law) for the "ugly man cake," in which men would bid in each others name, as the “ugly man.” During the course of the evening, I grew tired and bored of the festivities and went out to Dad’s car to relax. Thirteen-year-old Stella and her friend Loraine England came out and got in the back seat of the car. Their entire conversation was about boys! If I had been older, I might have been embarrassed, but as it was, I didn’t understand it, or care. Then Loraine looked at me and said to Stella, “I think I’ll just wait for your brother to grow up.” Now that meant that I was involved, so I got out of the car and went back in the school house.

Much of what Stella and her friends discussed had to do with boys from then on.

Stella first showed me the ridiculousness of the sense of false modesty forced on her by our mother when we went blackberry picking up on the Knob with some other kids. The girls were wearing slacks or shorts, but Stella wore a skirt. Soon she had rolled the top of the skirt in such a manner that almost all her thighs were exposed. I thought nothing of it, except that she looked a lot more comfortable.

Later Stella developed a close friendship with Jeanette Fleenor, who lived close to us. She was even younger than I, but they seemed to enjoy doing a lot of things together.

After she went to work at Oak Ridge she came home just about every third weekend, sometimes bringing co-workers with her. I considered them a bunch of silly girls—mostly because they liked to tease or kid me, me being at least a couple of years younger than they were. But sometimes they could also be a lot of fun. Our sister Ruth told Stella that she didn’t think I should be exposed to “girls like that,” whatever that meant. I saw them as not being a negative influence on me in any way.

On weekends when she did not return home, Stella and her friends seemed to spend a lot of time at Big Ridge Park, near Knoxville—swimming, sunbathing, picnicking. She seemed to have a plethora of boyfriends from that area, as well as relatives of her working friends. But nothing serious. Of course, most of them were in the military.

About boyfriends, I don't remember Stella ever having a date in high school. Henry Herron, later to be Ruth's husband, quite often rode his bicycle to our house for a visit. Coming with him sometimes was Ed Johnson—but he was not a date for Stella, although sometimes they did talk at length. After the war, she did date Ed's brother, Andy, a few times. One of the boys that seemed taken by her was Byrd Hensley, of Jonesville, the brother of one of her Oak Ridge co-workers, who was in the Navy. He even had her name tattooed on his arm, but she didn't really fancy him. She also dated a St. Charles boy named Junior Dickie a few times—who had not been in the military. But mostly she was with Roy Rutherford when he was home from the Navy.

Roy was a big galoot, football and baseball player, friend of our cousin, Howard. He tended to look down his nose at my brother and me—the kid brothers of his girlfriend. We thought he was snobbish. One day he and Stella were taking pictures in our front yard at Elk Knob, and Bee and I were out there. Roy was trying to get rid of us. Bee's big dog, Old Chief, was standing behind Roy. Bee picked up a rather chewed-up baseball bat with which he played fetch with the dog, and threw it over Roy's head. Old Chief wheeled, charging right onto Roy's legs, sending him almost into a somersault in mid-air—nice blue Navy uniform and all. We couldn't resist laughing, and neither could Stella. Soon after that Roy's brother, Harold, whom Stella had also dated, was killed in the Navy in the war, and she would have nothing to do with Roy either after that.

After she went to work at Collins Radio in Cedar Rapids, she developed a host of friends, some of whom I met. One interesting character was an old bachelor test technician who worked near her. One day she asked him why he never got married.

"I was always looking for the perfect woman," he answered.

"And you never found her?" said Stella, condescendingly.

"Oh yeah, I found her," he said, with a droll smirk. "But she was looking for the perfect man!"

Everybody around him howled.

About Brad Johnson; many years later, long after Stella's husband and Brad's wife had passed on, Stella was back in Lee County visiting our sister, when she and Brad got together—much to our sister's chagrin. Brad and Evelyn had lived in Noblesville, Indiana, for most of their marriage, as did many other people from our home area. But after Evelyn died, he had moved back, and worked as a mechanic at a local Pennington garage. He and Stella exchanged communications for a while, then she told me he called her one night, obviously he had been drinking, and begged her to get together with him—said he was getting old, and needed someone to take care of him. She reminded him that she had taken care of a sick man through most of her marriage, and certainly didn't need any more of that. She never talked to Brad again.

## Chapter 5, STELLA'S HUSBAND

On my first Sunday after discharge from the Navy I was sitting on our front porch at Elk Knob with Stella. Eventually our discussion led to the opposite sex. I told her I had nobody—had not even written to any girls except her during my Navy service, figuring the ones I knew would all be paired off by the time I came home. She told me she had a boy friend, maybe.

“Do you remember Ken Hedgecoth of Kemmerer Gem?” she asked.

“Yeah,” I said. “But he would be a little old for you, wouldn’t he?”

“He’s about eight years or so older than I am, but that’s a good thing.”

Then she told me there was a problem—he had bought a pickup truck.

My discerning look brought a laugh and an explanation. He was someone we had known as kids, although he was older. He had spent five years in the Army, but now lived in a coal camp with his folks, and worked in a mine. He came to see her quite often, and they had dates, but she never saw him alone. The other young people in the camp were so bored that every time he cranked up his truck to go somewhere, many of them ran and jumped in. She said that the previous Sunday they had planned a picnic trip to the Natural Tunnel, but he showed up with a truck bed full of people. Not only that, but one of the girls had her cap set for him, and pretended illness so she could ride in the front of the truck on the way back. His sister decided to ride up front to help the “sick” one, and my sister had to ride in the back with the rest of the herd.

When I asked if she had discussed this with him, she said yes, but he replied that they were his friends, and he didn’t want to insult them. She said she thought he was just too mealy-mouthed to talk to them about it. Then she told me I would see what she meant, because they had a date that afternoon. I told her it looked like only she could do something about it.

Sure enough, soon a one-ton Chevy flatbed pickup with a stock rack on it drove up to our front gate. There were two girls in the front seat with the driver, and six or eight young people in the bed. When the horn honked my sister didn’t move from the porch swing in which she was sitting. The driver came skipping down the front walk, and asked if she was ready.

I recognized the driver as being the guy she had told me about, Ken Hedgecoth, whom we had known as kids in Kemmerer Gem Coal Camp. I thought he was the skinniest man I had ever seen. In fact later I saw him once without his shirt, and he looked downright emaciated. You could count his ribs. He never changed.

Much to his obvious dismay, today she told him she was not going. She told him she thought she had a date with him, not with half the people in the coal camp. Grimly, he stalked back to his truck, and, wheels spinning, zoomed away.

"I still say he's a little old for you." I said.

"No, I don't think so," she replied. "He's eight or nine years older than I am. At least he is a man. So many boys I went to high school with never got over it. Some even quit school to join the military as soon as they turned seventeen. Now that they are home, they want to participate in high school stuff. I'm beyond that. I'm twenty-one, for heaven's sake! And Ken, who didn't finish high school, is way beyond it."

"Makes sense," I said. "But you might not ever see him again."

"Then I'll know if he really liked me," she said.

Later, while she was doing the Sunday dinner dishes, the truck came back—with just the driver in it. He was cheerful and friendly when he asked me to tell her he was there. She came out and they left.

The next Saturday he came back by our house, with his younger brother, James, a year younger than I, in his truck. I knew James, since he and I had played as small children in Kemmerer Gem.

"We're driving down to Spartansburg for a load of peaches," Ken said. "Want to go along, and help with the driving?"

Being bored, I went. The plan was to drive down to Spartansburg that day, which was right in the middle of the peach picking season, load the truck up with about a hundred bushels of peaches that night, then drive back overnight. The peaches were known as "culls" by the peach people—ones that would not be bought by the big canning companies—and could be purchased in bulk for a quarter to fifty-cents per bushel. The peaches could be hauled loose in the rack bed of the truck, then sold to coal camp women very cheap, a dollar to a dollar and a quarter a bushel, when they brought their own baskets. It looked like a pretty good racket to me. Later I wondered why Ken didn't make more trips.

A few days later I learned why—he showed up in a late model Plymouth, for which he had traded the pickup truck. Good decision!

I saw quite a bit of Ken and Stella during their courtship over the next six months, as I tried to get a handle on my own life. But right after Christmas I caught the bus to Dayton, where I could attend school on the G.I. Bill, while working in a factory. A few weeks later, I got a call from Stella. Our Bonny Blue grandmother had died, and she had requested that her grandsons be pallbearers. So I caught the bus back to Pennington. That's when I learned that Stella and Ken planned to marry in a couple of weeks. They wanted me to be there, but I didn't make it. A bus turned over on a mountain in Kentucky on the way down, and the one I was riding had to play rescuer. By the time I got home, Stella and Ken had married and were gone.

They settled in Keokee, where Ken got a job in a mine—and they bought a house, then had two sons. Then Ken got sick, and couldn't work. Things went down hill fast for them after that. Eventually I became instrumental in getting her a good job in Cedar Rapids, where I had moved to.

Ken got along great, caring for their two pre-schoolers and their home. Then one night Stella called me in desperation—Ken had passed out. I rushed to their home, called an ambulance, and got him in the local hospital. A series of tests revealed that he had a thyroid imbalance in his system, and needed further care. So we got him registered at the Veteran Administration Hospital in Iowa City, which was connected to the University of Iowa Hospital complex.

After several days, they told him that he had an over-active thyroid gland, which was screwing up the calcium deposits in his body. The VA doctors proposed that they remove part of his thyroid gland, to reduce its activity, but they would deliberately take too much than he would have to take thyroid medicine the rest of his life. There was no hesitation on the part of him or Stella in approving their suggestion. When the VA doctors operated, they found a tumor the size of a marble on his thyroid, and removed it. That was his trouble all along. A couple of weeks later they told him he was fine, to go get a job.

So a smiling Ken did—on second shift, like Stella, in final assembly in a company that manufactured portable rock crushers. Before long, they had bought a nice house and a brand new car. Then they decided to take their toddlers on their first vacation back to Virginia since moving away. Although they had planned to be gone two weeks, they returned in less than a week. Stella told us Ken said they were never going back again. His family had treated them like dirt. Just couldn't stand the idea of them being proud of doing better—with the new car, house, clothes and all.

Then one night Stella called to tell me Ken had a heart attack, and was in the hospital. I went to see him. The house they had bought was on four connected city lots, a small acreage really, and was loaded with garden spaces, fruit trees, grapevines and outbuildings. Ken loved spending his days working around there. He had simply overdone. While I was in his hospital room his doctor came in and talked to him about cutting back on his activities.

Stella said, “Why he won’t. He’ll be right back in here.”

“No he won’t,” said the doctor. “His next heart attack will put him somewhere else, not in the hospital.”

Ken got a bit big-eyed at that remark. A short time later they sold their place and bought a nice split-foyer house on the edge of a lighted golf course. Ken’s new hobby became restoring old cars—starting with a pickup truck.

As time went on, we moved to Cedar Falls, where the Hedgecoths used to visit us sometimes. Their two sons and mine liked to camp out in the back yard in a tent in summer, and in winter would bribe me to drive them to a Blackhawks hockey game by washing my car, or something. Then after a couple of years, we moved to a Chicago suburb, where they continued to visit us from time to time, taking in the local museums, zoos and such.

Then one day, while I was in Michigan City, Indiana, on business, I was called to the telephone of the company I was visiting. It was a distraught Stella. She was calling from a hospital in Kingsport, Tennessee. They had finally decided to visit down home again, now that their boys were teenagers, and Ken had gotten sick. He had become paralyzed from the waist down. She wanted my help. I reminded her that Ken had three brothers and one brother-in-law in that area. Why couldn’t they help? She said they had all run around like chickens with their heads cut off when Ken got sick, then disappeared. She couldn’t find any of them.

When I inquired further about Ken’s illness, she told me the Kingsport doctors said there was nothing physically wrong with him, that it was all psychosomatic—in his head. She said she had called his doctor back in Cedar Rapids, and he told her the doctors might be right, but he’d like to see for himself—and asked if she could get Ken to the Cedar Rapids hospital. That's when she called me.

I drove the hundred miles back home, then caught a plane out of O'Hare for Kingsport. But first I called Wathan Flying Service, where I once worked part time, in Cedar Rapids, and got prices and a schedule for a charter flight to bring Ken back. It was more reasonable than I thought.

When I entered Ken's room at the hospital, one of his younger brothers, an itinerant preacher, was bending over Ken's bed telling him he was going to die. Being already upset for having to be there, I grabbed the brother by the arms, telling him that Ken had enough troubles without that, and threatened to drop him over the stair railing. He retreated, and I never saw him again.

The next morning the hospital attendants packed Ken in a litter on the airplane, and I got ready to fly back home. But Stella insisted that I fly back to Cedar Rapids with Ken—while she and her boys drove back. I told her one of the boys should go with him, and she and the other could drive back. She wouldn't hear of it. So she called their best friends in Cedar Rapids, asked them to have an ambulance meet the plane, and I boarded the small single-engine charter for the long boring flight to Cedar Rapids. Ken's Cedar Rapids doctor found an aneurism in one of his legs, which had caused the paralysis. It was removed, and Ken went back to work. Eventually he died of a heart attack many years later.

## Chapter 6, STELLA'S FAMILY

Stella May Young had three siblings, plus a baby brother stillborn between her and her older sister, Gladys Ruth. Her two brothers were me, named Ishmael at birth, later Allan Ishmael; and L.B., given initials only at birth, a common practice in our part of the country, (we called him "Bee,") later Lincoln Brett. Ruth was three years older than Stella, I was three years younger, then Bee was two years younger than I was.

After moving to Iowa she always seemed so happy to have gotten her sons to a place where they would not want for anything.

Stella and Ken had two sons, Marvin Dale and Norman Allan; plus four grandsons and three grand daughters. She had many great grandchildren—and she was the rock in everybody's lives. She deplored some situations in which they were involved, but still understood what had happened, and could accept the human weaknesses of her family members.

No one knew the depths of her distress when two of her grandsons died. Her first one passed away in his crib when just a few days old—one of those unexplainable crib deaths that happen to infants sometimes. The other one, Joel, was thirteen, and playing at a neighbor kid's house, when his playmate pulled his dad's shotgun out of a closet, pointed it at Joel, and pulled the trigger. The gun was loaded. In both of these situations, Stella was too busy doing things for the survivors—fixing food, comforting people, showing strength—for anybody to read her feelings, although I knew she was devastated.

## Chapter 7, STELLA'S ILLNESSES

During those early years at Elk Knob, we four kids got all kinds of childhood ailments—chicken pox, measles, mumps, whooping cough. Then Stella came down with something serious; diphtheria. The coal company doctor came all the way to our house, several times. Sister Ruth and I were quarantined at home—couldn't go to school. Little brother Bee hadn't started school yet. I remember being so sorry for Stella who had no proper night clothes. She lay in bed all day and night wearing the cutoff top of long-handle underwear and baggy bloomers. I hated for the doctor, who visited every day, to see her like that. Even then, her biggest fear was not for herself, but that she would give it to some of the rest of us.

I was so glad when she got over it, in time to go kite-flying with me—one of our favorite spring pastimes.

During this period, Stella was starting to grow up, and one of her bodily changes became the need for glasses. Nobody in my family wore glasses yet. She was the first. I thought she might be embarrassed, but she was not. Wanted to see better, I guess. Dad dropped her and me off in Pennington on his way to work, so we had to kill time until the eye doctor opened his office. We had no appointment, but I guess nobody did. No telephones.

After her exam we were to simply walk the five miles home. Nothing new, we had done it before. As we left town we had to walk under a railroad overpass, and a man was sitting alongside the road there. Stella walked right at him. At the last minute I grabbed her by the arm and steered her around him. With the eye drops still blurring her sight, she simply had not seen him! I hung onto her the rest of the way home.

After Stella moved to Iowa she started to put on weight, so she started smoking—as her husband always had. I think she thought it might help her lose weight. It didn't. Later, after she quit, she told me how much better everything tasted.

I do not remember her having any day-to-day illnesses, until she got older and started to have replacement joints installed. She had one knee, one shoulder, and one hip replaced—and had the other shoulder scheduled to be replaced when she died.

Her oldest son, Dale, jokingly called her "Stainless Steel Stella."

When he called me a few months before she died to tell me had gone to visit his mother and found her fallen on the kitchen floor in a pool of blood from a head injury, I worried.

Then he told me she was not the "same old Stella" anymore. I talked to her often on the phone after that, and she seemed normal to me.

I was saddened when he called to tell me she was no longer with us.

Chapter 8, STELLA'S JOBS

The Monday after she graduated from high school Stella had packed her meager belongings into a cheap suitcase and caught the bus to Knoxville, then on to Oak Ridge, where she had heard some new government project was hiring people. When they told her it would take a couple of weeks for her to be processed and hired, she did not head back home. She rented a sleeping room, and got a job in a textile mill in Knoxville, as a night janitor—cleaning up after the day workers spent the day sewing.

But soon she was working at Oak Ridge, not really knowing what she was doing. She and hundreds of girls like her were stationed in front of a long panel of dials and control knobs, with the assignment of twisting the knobs in the right way to keep the dials reading to pre-assigned levels. She liked the work, and since they all worked swing shifts, every three weeks she had a seventy-two hour break. That is when she would usually come home for a visit.

Her income was not all that great, but she was a lot of help to her parents and siblings. When she learned I needed a new suit, for which my own meager income from odd jobs, could not afford, she insisted that she buy it for me. Later, when I went into the Navy, she was the only girl I wrote to.

During her first summer at Oak Ridge, she invited me down to look for a temporary job. I found nothing, because I was only sixteen years old, having just finished my junior year of high school—and no one would hire me. It never occurred to me to lie about my age, although I could have passed for eighteen, and few people had birth certificates at that time.

Stella dressed well, having an affinity for shoes and purses, especially if they matched. I had always thought of her as more mature than her age, but during these Oak Ridge years, I saw her as more grown up than ever. She certainly looked great in her clothes, or out of them, in shorts and swim suits.

I enlisted in the Navy right out of high school, and didn't see her again until I was discharged. When I came home, she was home, having just been let go from her job—now that the war was over. Soon I headed for Dayton, for jobs of my own. Then she and Ken got married.

With my own life in Dayton, I didn't see much of them for quite some time. Ken had gone to work in a mine at Keokee, they had bought a house there, and had two sons. But in the summer of 1950 I got a letter from Stella telling me that Ken had gotten ill, and not only was unable to work, but had been told by the Pennington hospital doctors that he would never be able to work again. Pretty harsh, I thought at the time. You can always work at something, if you can find it.

In the letter she was asking if perhaps she could get a job in Dayton. I wrote back, saying that there were many factories in Dayton, and most were hiring constantly. Even though we had a very small house, and had one child, I invited her to come stay with us temporarily—at least until she could get a job and get established—that she could sleep on our couch. We were expecting our second child soon, which would complicate the arrangement, but by then she should be okay. I told her I couldn't be of much help—I was working seven days a week as a designer in a tool and die job shop—so she would have to ride the bus everywhere around Dayton.

She called to tell me what time she would arrive one evening, so I could meet her at the Greyhound station. When she got off the bus, our mother was with her! I wasn't prepared for that. When I bluntly asked Mom what she was doing there, she said that my dad had insisted that she come. I knew they had been having trouble for years, but I didn't believe her. Knowing my mother's impulsive ways, I figured she had just invited herself along for the trip. I told them we didn't have anyplace for two people to sleep—one, but not two. I dug up a thin mattress for someone to sleep on the floor.

My mother stayed, I think, two nights, then caught the bus back home—following with a nasty letter about she was not welcome in my home, which hurt Rosemary's feelings. I just laughed it off. I wasn't in the business of welcoming visitors—just trying to help Stella get a job. After she had applied at several factories, but none had called her back yet, I came home from work one night to find her all packed and ready to catch the bus back home. Ken had called to tell her she had a job in St. Charles. Before coming to Dayton she had applied for jobs at several businesses around home to no avail, but now the Miners' Store—a long-standing clothing establishment—had offered her a clerking job if she wanted it. So she had decided it was what would be better—no move involved.

By the time our father died the following spring our second child was four months old, and I was making plans for a move. I had gone to work at Wright-Patterson Air Force Base in January, and had made contact with Collins Radio Company in Cedar Rapids, one of our fast growing suppliers. They wanted me to come for an interview. Since neither Rosemary nor I had thought of Dayton as a permanent place to live and raise our kids, we decided to pursue it. Shortly after we returned to Dayton from Dad's funeral, we began a move to Cedar Rapids, based on the job interview I had previously arranged. We drove out for the interview and I accepted their offer of a job, then leaving Rosemary and the kids at her folks' farm, a hundred miles west of Cedar Rapids, I went back to Dayton alone to make the move.

I had learned during our visit to Dad's funeral that Ken and Stella had really gotten hard up. They had lost their house and their car, and had moved in with Ken's parents. Her job at the store paid only fourteen dollars a week, so she told me she was begging milk from neighbors who had cows to feed her little boys. Thinking about this, and remembering her job at Oak Ridge, as soon as I was settled into my job as tool designer in the manufacturing engineering department at Collins I went to see the personnel manager about Stella. When he told me they would hire her in a minute into a good paying test technician's position, I wrote her a letter, and sent her a job application.

I had no idea how she would react. I thought maybe at best she might come out to Cedar Rapids for a visit, to look things over. We had no phone, so I waited to hear from her by mail. We were surprised a few nights later to have a cab driver knock on our door at the farm tenant house we rented out in the country, asking if that was the Allan Young residence. Stella and her family were with him. They had sold everything they owned, except their clothing, and had taken the 800-mile train trip to a new beginning!

Again, as our small abode already housed four people, it would be tight to add another four, but in a desperate situation, you make do—and we did. They were really starting over—with no furniture, no car, none of the basic things a family needs to exist. But both Stella and her husband exuded cheerfulness. I guess when you've been to the bottom anyway you go is up. She pitched right in to help Rosemary, and inquired about the small house trailer our landlord had sitting near our house. I knew nothing about it, except that it was unoccupied. The next day I asked him about it. He said it was as fully furnished as such things usually are, but they would have to have bedclothes and such. However, he would rent it really cheap.

On my next work day, a Monday, Stella rode into Cedar Rapids with me, carrying her filled-out job application. She came into my work area later to tell me that she had been hired, but that it would take the personnel department about two weeks to process her references and such. She wanted to know if maybe she could get a job in a downtown store for that time, based on her retail experience. I couldn't leave, but I told her where to catch a bus downtown. When I came out of the plant later that day, she was waiting for me. She had been hired by Woolworth's five and dime, and was to start working the very next day. We worked out a schedule, whereby she would ride to Collins with me every morning, then catch the bus from there to the downtown area, since I had to be at work before her store opened, then I would drive down to Woolworth's after work, getting there just about the time they closed. Her job was low pay, and had no benefits, but it would work as a stop-gap measure.

A couple of weeks later she was in Collins beginners training program, and soon thereafter was a test technician on the second shift, checking communications equipment at a sit-down job in a wire enclosure, which blocked out electronic interference. By then she had rented the trailer, bought necessary supplies for it, and she and Ken were thinking of buying a used car—so they would not be so dependent on me for transportation. They knew we were hoping to buy a house in town. I was thinking what a difference a good income can make, and almost immediately.

Stella worked at that Collins Radio job until she retired.

## Chapter 9, STELLA'S HOMES

The first time my wife Rosemary and I visited Stella's home was right after we were engaged to be married, and I had escorted my fiancée to Lee County to meet the members of my family. Stella and Ken lived in a little three-room house in Kemmerer Gem coal camp. They had been married just a few months and had no children yet. In the course of our initial conversation it was brought out that Rosemary was Catholic.

Ken turned to Stella and said, “Would you have married me if I had been a Catholic?”

“Honey I would have married you even if you were a cannibal!” said Stella, to the laughter of all of us.

Later Ken went to work at the Keokee mines, and they bought a house there. After Ken became unable to work, they moved to Bonny Blue, and then back to Kemmerer Gem to live with Ken’s parents. When they came to Iowa they lived in a small house trailer for a while, then a series of rental properties, until they bought their own home. After Ken died, Stella sold the house to buy a smaller one. We visited her there quite often, while our daughter Kay was in college in Cedar Rapids.

I liked to kid her there. Like the time I came to Cedar Rapids on business. I got her all excited by calling to tell her I was in the local jail, and needed her to come bail me out.

Once we were there when Kay had her nurse’s capping ceremony at the college. Many of Stella’s relatives were at her house, as were our son and his girlfriend. In the course of the visit I asked the girlfriend what she thought of all these people.

She sighed and said, “Everybody talks, but nobody listens!”

Later Stella sold that house to move back to Knoxville, Tennessee. We visited her there a couple of times, and the layer of smoke in the city was unbearable. It filled her apartment every time someone opened a door. She moved back to Cedar Rapids and bought another house, where she lived out her life.

## Chapter 10, STELLA’S WIDOWHOOD

Soon after her husband's death, Collins offered Stella early retirement, as they were doing for several people. She took it.

We enjoyed visiting with her during these years. Since our youngest daughter was in college in Cedar Rapids, Stella's home was a good stopping place. Also we enjoyed having her visit us after we moved back to southern Iowa, touring the river towns and going boating up to an island in the Mississippi which we leased.

On a subsequent vacation trip to Knoxville to visit old friends, she had became convinced to move there—after all those years away. That's when she sold her house in Cedar Rapids, and rented an apartment in Knoxville. Rosemary and I stopped to visit her there on our way back from visiting my mother in Kingsport one time. It was obvious she regretted the move. Our brother in Knoxville had remarried, so she didn't see much of him. Her old friends had their own lives, so had grown away from mutual interests. Our cousin, Howard, in Kingsport, wanted her to live with him—but she realized that he just wanted a cook and housekeeper. Besides, she had many grandchildren and great-grandchildren back in Cedar Rapids. Next thing we knew, she had moved back, and bought another house.

Then our mother died.

She had long ago sold the old Elk Knob place and made a permanent move to Kingsport. The Kingsport hospital called me one night to tell me our mother had been brought there in a coma. She had resided for a long time in a senior citizens' apartment, where each resident was required to put a bouquet of artificial flowers on the outside of the door each morning, to let the staff know they were all right. The apartment manager had long ago told me that when a resident became ill, or died, sometimes their relatives would take all their belongings from their apartment. I had told her, in writing, that, being the executor of my mother's estate, if anything happened to her, no one was to be allowed in that apartment but me.

Our mother had a heart attack, and had been unconscious for twenty minutes before the ambulance picked her up. I talked to her doctor, and he said she was brain-dead, being kept alive by machines, but would never get better. We were in the process of moving to the Ozarks, so I told him I would not come to Kingsport until I had to. But I would talk to him every day.

I notified my siblings of the situation, and Stella, with her son and his wife, decided to drive to Kingsport. But after a few days with no change, her son and his wife had to get back home to their jobs. Stella stayed on at Howard's place.

Then Howard called me to tell me that I had better get down there. A couple of my nieces had approached Howard to try to get into my mother's apartment, to "get some things." They had even backed a pickup truck up to the place, but the manager wouldn't let them in. So Rosemary and I went. After talking to the doctor at length, I suggested that he unplug the machines. He wanted me to sign a form, which I got Stella and our sister Ruth to sign also. Soon our mother was gone. Stella, Howard, Rosemary and I went through our mother's stuff. The apartment manager knew people who would buy the furniture and haul the clothing to the Salvation Army. We kept some things out for Ruth, and Stella took a few things. Rosemary and I took nothing.

Now Stella had a dilemma. She had some things to get back to Cedar Rapids, including a library table. I bit the bullet, and told her that if she would buy me an eighty dollar top carrier for my car, I would drive the 500 miles out of my way to take her to Cedar Rapids. That's what we did. I'm sure she appreciated it.

The following year I added a screen porch to our house. When our Cedar Rapids friends visited, he said he would really like to have such a porch. So when Rosemary and her sister decided to fly to California for a week to visit their brothers, I called my friend and told him if he was serious about the porch, I would come up during that week and build him one. This I did.

On the third day of construction, our friend invited Stella over for supper. As she walked past our ongoing work, she almost snarled that she thought we would be further along than we were. She kept that up through supper—so unlike her. I decided something must be eating on her, causing her to have a bad day.

I turned to my hosts and said, "You know, folks, I believe you have invited the wrong person to supper."

Stella almost collapsed in her chair, saying, "Oh my god, I sound just awful, don't I?"

Then her attitude got better. I never did know what was wrong with her.

Later we discussed building a screen porch on her house, but I discouraged it, knowing that it would be for the next owners. I didn't want to be caught in the same situation a friend of mine was. He spent all his weekends for a year building his father and mother a house. After they moved in, his dad had an opportunity to sell the house for a lot of money, and did. That friend cried on my shoulder that his dad was selling his son's free labor, so he wouldn't do anything for his dad after that.

Eventually Stella became unable to drive, so she sold her car. She had enough friends and relatives in Cedar Rapids to get her where she wanted to go.

Then her oldest son called to tell me he had come to visit her, and found her lying on the kitchen floor in a pool of blood. He got her all taken care of, and in a nursing home temporarily. Later he told me she was different now, but when I would call her, she sounded normal.

I was saddened when Dale called to tell me she was no longer with us.

None of her siblings were at her funeral. The distance was over 800 miles for both Brett and our sister Ruth, and over 500 miles for me. Mine and Rosemary's sixty-year-old son and his wife drove out to Cedar Rapids from their home in the Chicago area to represent us at the funeral. Many people thought he was me. (Either he looked like an octogenarian, or they thought I was much younger!)

Epilogue, EULOGIES

When Stella died, her oldest grandson, John Hedgecoth; our brother, Lincoln Brett Young; and I were asked to contribute eulogies, which John would read at her funeral. Here are the eulogies for Stella May Young Hedgecoth.

JOHN HEDGECOTH:

When Stella brought her family here from coal country on the train in 1953 as Allan wrote about, the family didn't have a lot of stuff. Just a few suitcases. But what she was bringing with her, can't be put inside a suitcase.

She brought with her the delicious southern family recipes. I have ordered cole slaw in restaurants around this country and never had any as good as hers. And we all were offered the sweet tea made out in the sun. Raise your hand if you can remember Stella offering you a glass of tea.

She brought with her the family musical traditions of the south. We actually used to sit around in a circle and listen to guitar, banjo, and singing late into the night. And no, the circle won't be broken. You know, I was about thirteen before I realized not everyone's family had sing-alongs at holidays. And she always had to hear "Rocky Top" before it was over.

She brought with her a manner, a way to communicate that she cared, that was as endearing and expressive as it was straight out of east Tennessee. As a grandchild, when you went to Grandma with an accomplishment, like for me, finally getting on base in little league, she would respond by saying, "Well bless your heart." Those blessings meant everything when we were little.

And, she brought with her a steely determination that a better life was just up the road, that her sons wouldn't have to work in the mines, and that her entire family would feel cared for.

These are just a few of the things she brought with her. They say men define themselves by their careers and women by their relationships. Truly great people do both things well, and Stella was one of these.

You see, it took her nearly sixty years here in Iowa to unpack what all she brought with her. And we are still benefiting from and being inspired by all of it. So, today is our chance to say, Grandma Stella, we love you, and "bless your heart."

LINCOLN BRETT YOUNG ·

My favorite memory of my sister Stella is insignificant when compared to the other things she did, such as helping to usher in the Atomic Age and the Space Age.

It happened on a cold winter day when I was seven or eight years old and Stella was about twelve or thirteen. She had a huge book of fairy tales and nursery rhymes. We sat on the floor behind our little Heatrola coal stove, which was the warmest place in the house. For about two hours she read fairy tales and poems to me. I was so happy that she cared enough to spend that much time entertaining me that I have carried that memory for seventy years. Another event that comes to mind is when Stella graduated from high school. She was salutatorian of her graduating class. As such, she gave a speech at the graduation ceremony. She missed being valedictorian by about one grade point. She always maintained that a certain teacher gave the other student extra points that were not earned, thereby leaving Stella in second place. Later, I had that same hateful teacher, and I think she was fully capable of committing such an act.

After graduation, Stella left our little country home and went to Knoxville, Tennessee, to take a job in a cotton mill. She worked there a few months then got a better job in Oak Ridge. She and the other workers at Oak Ridge did not know what they were making. They were not allowed to talk to anyone about thcir work   not even to each other. Only after World War II ended did the workers learn that they had been creating atomic bombs. Just the scientists, a few generals, and top government officials knew.

While she worked at Oak Ridge our father became partially disabled because of black lung disease and an injury at work, so Stella sent money home for us to live on. This enabled me to finish high school. I'm not sure that I ever thanked her for that, so I'll do it now. Thank you, Stella, for all you have done for me and many other members of our family. You are a fine, kind person. All my love always.

ALLAN ISHMAEL YOUNG

My sister Stella was a sentimentalist, but with enough ingrained humor and mischief to keep those in her world happy. As a small girl in our home in Virginia the cats were hers, but when one of them died, she would bury it in a shoebox, then pick violets and daisies for days, putting them on its grave, while sitting there on the grass with tears in her big beautiful blue eyes. Yet in later years, suffering through the untimely deaths of her husband and two grandsons, she was a dependable rock of strength for the rest of the family, in spite of her own grief.

Even when she came down with diphtheria at age eleven, and we were all quarantined, with the doctor visiting every day, her biggest fear was not for herself, but that she would give it to some of the rest of us. Again, in later years, she cared for many friends and relatives through their sickness and injury without fail.

As a small child in a coal camp, Stella was always surrounded by a lot of close friends, a pattern which never changed. She accumulated more on through school, and for the rest of her life.

But as a young girl she would turn her serious nature upside down and let her mischief show. Once when I was about eight, she wanted me to accompany her somewhere that I didn't want to go. So she said she would give me a gift. When I asked her what, she said a pair of socks. Now we were poor, so the prospect of a new pair of socks was pleasing to a small boy. When we returned and I went to collect my socks, she socked me two times with her little fists. I got even with her soon after, knowing how easily frightened she was of the dark, I turned off the outside lights when she went to the outhouse. We laughed about both events well into our senior years.

I had begun to realize what a beautiful girl she was when she started high school. She always dressed as sharp as our circumstances allowed, and her naturally blond hair was always neatly cared for. After I started high school two years later, we were talking in the hall one day when one of the senior boys cornered me later. He asked me if I knew that pretty junior. When I said yes, he told me she was the most delightful and confident girl in school. He said he had been given the task of gathering a team of students and inventorying the books in the library. He said Stella had stepped in with enthusiasm, took over part of his load, and cheerfully helped until the job was done. She had the best grades in her class.

After our father was unable to work very much, our income was practically nil, but she had gone to work at Oak Ridge, and proceeded to help the family. When she learned I needed a new suit, for which my own meager income from odd jobs, could not buy, she insisted that she buy it for me. When I went into the Navy, she was the only girl I wrote to.

But her resolute toughness showed up when our economically depressed area offered no opportunities for her and her family to live a decent life. I had come to work at Collins as a tool designer, and I almost casually told her in a letter that I had discussed her with the personnel manager, who said they could use her, and I had sent her a job application. I had thought that perhaps she would come out and look things over, maybe take the job, then bring her family later. Not gutsy Stella! She loaded them all on the train, and came over 800 miles to Cedar Rapids to stay. And stay they did. After her husband's health improved, he got a job at Iowa Manufacturing, and they raised two boys to be proud of, and a whole flock of grandkids, of which she was proud, and rightfully so.

The Hedgecoth family has lost a strong rallying point, but their memory of her and her example, should last forever. I know mine will.

*I can truly say that my mother was a mountain of will that I have not seen before or since. When I think of her I think of strength.* Dale Hedgecoth

THE END

# Part II
# RUTH'S STORY

RUTH'S STORY, by Allan Ishmael Young

## Chapter 1, RUTH'S CHILDHOOD

Gladys Ruth Young was born on June 30, 1922 at Black Mountain, Virginia, a coal camp, to a seventeen-year-old mother and a twenty-seven-year-old coal miner father. Her parents had to learn all their parenting skills on raising her, before her sister and three brothers arrived. Their second child, one of the boys, was stillborn.

Little Ruth made few friends in the coal camp, and was somewhat sheltered by her young mother, who kept her well-dressed and entertained. All that changed as her siblings arrived, as their mother got too busy to devote much time to one child. But Ruth learned to read at an early age, and kept herself entertained with books.

My sister Ruth was put upon, teased and picked on for her entire life, by family, friends and loved ones. She had the patience of Job, and let the derogatory statements go in one ear and out the other. Even the unpleasant activities of those around her had no obvious negative effect on her. She was able to accept them and let them pass.

## Chapter 2, RUTH'S SCHOOL DAYS

The only one of us kids to have the opportunity to go to kindergarten, Ruth entered at the St. Charles school. Since we lived at Penn Lee coal camp at the time, she had to walk with the other kids on a curvy mountain blacktop road about a mile to school. Along the way in winter there were icicles hanging from the bluffs by the road. Against her parents' warnings, she ate some of the ice. When her mother asked her how her gloves got wet, she told her she had washed her hands with her gloves on.

Being poor and gullible, when some of the other kids convinced her that one of the stores in St. Charles was giving away free candy, she went there at lunch time and asked for some. The other kids had hidden to laugh at her. Similar events happened to her in her early years of school, even after the family moved to Kemmerer Gem coal camp, where she attended a one-room school.

She was fourteen years old when we moved to Elk Knob, and she attended that school. It was still a high school at that time, but became a grade school only, when the new high school was built at Pennington. On the first day she was to attend there, for some unexplainable reason our parents kept Ruth home the first day—waiting until things were established at the new school, was all they said. I thought it was a mistake, because Ruth wound up behind all the other kids in scheduling and just finding her way around. I'm sure it affected her studies.

During these years a summer teaching/recreational program was started at the Elk Knob school, which Ruth seemed to enjoy. She made several friends there, and one boy in particular. More on that later.

I do not know what kind of student she was, because we never attended Pennington High together, but she seemed to enjoy biology, as well as French, one of the two foreign languages offered at the school—if Latin could be considered a foreign language.

By the time Ruth graduated she was in a thick relationship with Henry Herron of Kemmerer Gem, who bought her an elaborate dresser set as a graduation gift. She seemed so pleased with it that four years later, when I graduated, I bought a smaller one for a favorite girl as a graduation gift.

## Chapter 3, RUTH'S ENTERTAINMENT

Except for going places with our Aunt Dixie and Uncle John, Ruth's only other outside entertainment was attending church with our mother and Stella.

But Ruth liked to cook and sew. She especially liked to bake cakes and pies. Sometimes these were disasterous, but she took it all in stride. Once she baked what she called a “fudge cake,” and my brother and I told her it really “fudged.” It exploded right up the middle, leaving a gaping hole in it. She just calmly filled the hole with chocolate fudge, as well as putting a layer of the sweet stuff all over the rest of the cake. We boys ate it like there was no tomorrow.

After she was married, her husband and kids didn’t like desserts, but she would bake some for us brothers sometimes. Once I came in her front door and was negotiating for a chocolate pie she had baked, which was cooling on her back porch. She wanted me to do some work for her in exchange for the pie. After we settled on a list of chores, we were both chagrined to learn that my brother had come up on the back porch, and was eating the pie. He had to do the chores.

During her first years at Elk Knob a 4-H Club was formed there. It was right up Ruth’s alley. More cooking and sewing of a formal nature, with instruction. Ruth made dresses and aprons out of feed sacks, and other discarded material—sewing them on our mother’s treadle-type sewing machine. Right about this time Ruth decided she should be wearing a brassiere, but our mother would not buy her one. She said girls should not emphasize parts of their bodies—and she and none of her friends wore them. Ruth simply made herself one. I do not know how she figured it out, but it was nice, and it worked. Later she made one for Stella as well.

## Chapter 4, RUTH’S FRIENDS

In each school Ruth attended, she seemed to cultivate one close friend. At Kemmerer Gem it was Myrtle Green, and at Elk Knob it was Hazel Bates. I do not remember much about Myrtle, except that she had a sister my age named Delsey, whom I liked.

Hazel carried her lunch, and would walk to our house with Ruth, eating as she went. One day there was a dead cat in the road. Hazel threw her remaining sandwich at the cat, and continued on down the road. She did that every day for a few days, until the cat was devoured by buzzards. (After she grew up and her family moved to Kingsport, Hazel dated, then married, a guy named Earl Cookenour—whom she jokingly called "Earl Cook-a-turd-a-half-an-hour" to Ruth and other friends.)

While we still lived in Kemmerer Gem, a boy Ruth's age, named Claude Fultz, became fond of her. She couldn't stand him—especially since he insisted on calling her "Wifey" in front of other kids.

During the summer program at the Elk Knob school, Ruth became friends with a boy named Ralph Hobbs, and they did everything in the program together. A little red-headed girl who couldn't talk very plain was in the program, and she called the young couple "Ouch and Ooch," her words for "Ralph and Ruth."

One day I heard her say, "Ouch and Ooch! Every where I look, I see Ouch and Ooch."

Shortly after this, Henry Herron, son of one of my father's best friends in Kemmerer Gem, started riding his bicycle clear from the coal camp to our house almost every Sunday afternoon. He came to see Ruth. But she was still spending several week days with Ralph.

Our mother objected to that, saying, "You just can't be going with two boys."

Stella and I saw nothing wrong with it, and voiced our opinions. But our mother just got mad at us. She deplored the fact that Ralph didn't have a regular job—he just did farm work for several people. Henry had quit school at age sixteen to go to work with his father in the coal mine. Then when Henry gave Ruth that fancy dresser set for graduation that sealed the deal for our mother—Ruth could only go with him. Poor Mom—our Dad was the only boy she had ever even spoken to, so she knew nothing about dating.

Of course, I liked it when Henry came, because I didn't have a bicycle, and I could ride his all the time he was there. Many times a friend of his would also ride along with Henry, ostensibly to visit Stella, which she didn't like. That was okay, too, because now my brother also had a bike to ride.

About the time Ruth graduated from high school, Henry's father bought some land west of our place about a half-mile, and built a fairly large house on it, complete with smoke house, garage, hog pen and wash house—where he and Henry could also take a bath after working all day in a coal mine with no bathing facilities.

I spent quite a bit of time there with Henry's brothers, playing Rook, a card game, or just visiting. I was there when Henry answered his call to be drafted, and heard his mother tell him to be sure to join the "Standin' Army," whatever she thought that was. Henry failed the physical for the military.

As a follow-up, Ralph joined the Army and stayed until he retired. Burbee Johnson, Bradley's older brother, who lived across the road from us at Elk Knob, wrote to Ruth after he joined the Army—but by then she had married Henry.

Years later, after Ruth had been a widow for a long time, she blurted out to me once that she had always thought much more of Ralph Hobbs than of Henry.

## Chapter 5, RUTH'S HUSBAND

I came in the house one Saturday for lunch and my mother was cooking over the coal stove with tears in her eyes. I could recall seeing her cry only one time before, so it was strange to me. On my inquiry of her, she finally said that Ruth and Henry had gone to St. Charles to get married. I learned later that they had wanted to be married by a Preacher Green of the Baptist

Church, so Henry's father had driven them up there. Green had some service going, and when it was over, he came out to their car, and since it was raining, got in the vehicle with them, and performed the marriage service in the car. They moved into Henry's room at his folks' house, until they could get their own place and furniture.

Soon after they were married, Henry bought a motorcycle. It seemed incongruous to me that a young married man with a baby on the way would do that, instead of buying a car—until I learned that he wanted to buy one while still single, but his mother wouldn't let him.

Henry worked as a coal digger at Kemmerer Gem, but wanted to try other things—so, since others were going other places to do defense work, he tried it, too. First he tried Detroit, but didn't stay. Then he went to Baltimore, where our cousin Harry offered to help him. Harry said he loaned Henry his second car, so he could get around the city, seeking employment. One evening, on his way home from work, Harry said he saw his car sitting beside the road, out of gas. Henry had run it out of fuel, and just walked away. Soon after Harry quit helping him, Henry went back home to Elk Knob.

When I lived in Dayton, I got a letter from my mother, telling me that Ruth and Henry, with their three daughters, had moved to that city. She had their address, but they had no phone. She hadn't been able to connect with them, and worried. I decided to drive to the address, which was a furnished apartment.

When one of the girls let me in, I found Ruth eating popcorn. There was no other food in the house, and their landlord had ordered them to move out the next day, for non-payment of rent. Henry had a car that wouldn't run, but no job. Ruth told me that if she could just get back to her house at Elk Knob she would be okay.

Seeing the desperate situation, I took her and the girls home with me. Although we had two babies in a very small house, I thought we could make out somehow overnight. Then I took Henry to where he had left his car. I soon realized that car was never going to run without major repair. It was mid-winter, and all the wiring and such was frozen and broken. When I asked Henry if he had enough money to fix it, he told me he had seven dollars. I took him back to our place, and prepared for a 350-mile drive to Virginia.

We drove across Kentucky in a blizzard, with me sweating blood all the way. I got them home early in the morning, went to my mother's place for a two-hour nap, then headed back to Dayton. Mom was much chagrined that I would not drive on down to Knoxville to visit my father, a patient at Fort Sanders VA hospital. Back in Dayton I had a wife and two small children in a house with a faulty heating system, from which I could not be gone very long.

Henry went back to work in the coal mines, and Ruth had a fourth child, a son.

Many years later, Stella and her husband, feeling good about their successes in Cedar Rapids, wanted to do something to help Ruth and Henry. They brought him out there, where he rented an apartment, and got a job driving the city bus. His boss liked him so well that they became fishing buddies. But before Ruth could join him there, he screwed up again, and found himself back in Elk Knob. Soon after that, he had an eye damaged in the mine, and was retired on a disability pension.

Henry died fairly young, and we went to his funeral—at the old Station Creek Church, where my father's funeral had been held. There were so many flowers there that we determined that Ruth could have lived well for quite a while on that investment, if the money had been given to her.

## Chapter 5, RUTH'S FAMILY

Ruth had four children, the first three of them girls—Joy, Brenda and Faye. Randy was the boy's name. When the first one was born, the visitors were discussing who the baby looked like. Henry's grandmother said that it didn't look like anybody she had ever seen. Our mother blew up, thinking that the old lady meant to infer that the baby was not Henry's. But then Henry's folks were like that.

Ruth's son seemed to have inherited some of his dad's musical talent. As a young man at our mother's funeral he played some organ pieces, and I hoped he would play more. Ruth's daughter and her family had a musical group, and Ruth wanted them to take over the music at our mother's funeral. As executor of our mother's estate, I said no. I told them they could add to the services, but I would not cancel anything. Mom had given me, in writing, a year before she died, complete instructions for the service—depicting the minister, the pallbearers, the musicians. I had given a copy of this to all my siblings.

I learned also that two of her daughters drove a truck up to Mom's apartment, planning to clean it out while Mom was in the hospital, brain dead. Of course, the apartment manager would not let them in.

After I instructed the doctor, with the approval of Stella and Ruth, to unplug the support from our mother—who had been living by machines pumping blood and oxygen through her body, never to recover—Ruth asked me if I was guilty of euthanasia. I felt insulted, but just considered the source of the question, and let it pass.

## Chapter 7, RUTH'S ILLNESSES

Besides the usual childhood diseases, to my knowledge, Ruth never suffered any illnesses as a young girl and woman. After she became a widow, I heard that she had a mastectomy for breast cancer, but she never communicated that to me.

## Chapter 8, RUTH'S JOBS

To my knowledge, Ruth never held a job outside her home. After high school graduation, she went job-hunting at Kingsport—a town which was growing rapidly with defense plants. She lived with her friend Hazel Bates and her parents, who had moved there. But our mother went over to see her every couple of days, and eventually talked her into coming home—jobless. She tried selling some products door-to-door for a while, then married Henry—just to get away from our mother, I thought. I believed that Mom was a big thorn in Ruth's side her whole life—probably because they lived near each other.

## Chapter 9, RUTH'S HOMES

When Ruth and Henry first got married, his father arranged for him to buy the furniture of some coal camp couple who were divorcing. They then rented a small three-room house next to the Elk Knob school, where their first child was born. Later they rented a house in St. Charles to be closer to Henry's work. From there they moved to a house in Stone Creek.

Later they built a three-room house next door to Henry's parents at Elk Knob. They still had that place through all of Henry's attempts to move to various cities.

Eventually, long after our father died, our mother decided to sell our old home place at Elk Knob. Henry's parents had died, and their house was now owned by Henry's sister and her husband, who wanted to buy Ruth and Henry's place, too. So Henry and Ruth wanted to buy our mother's place, but she was mad at them, and wouldn't sell it to them.

As it came about, Mom's place had to be auctioned off by the bank, so Henry's brother-in-law bid on it, bought it, and traded it to Ruth and Henry for theirs. They lived there until

Henry died, and Ruth has lived there alone ever since.

Interesting—long after Ruth became a widow, in questioning how she was doing alone, she answered that she had people who shopped for her, then she blurted out that she had a man who did things around her house for her. I learned it was Ralph Hobbs!

THE END

SUMMARY

So there you have it, STELLA and RUTH, my sisters.

A down-in-the-dumps Stella dragged her semi-invalid husband 800 miles away for an opportunity which she hoped would work out. It did.

An upbeat Ruth followed her chosen husband wherever he wanted to go and live, hoping one would work out. None did, so they finally settled at their home in Elk Knob, where they were comfortable, to finish out their days.

Were they both happy with their choices?

I have no way of knowing!

THE END

www.ingramcontent.com/pod-product-compliance
Ingram Content Group UK Ltd.
Pitfield, Milton Keynes, MK11 3LW, UK
UKHW041840200726
13854UKWH00003BA/1232